GREEN LANTERN

VOLUME 5 TEST OF WILLS

HARSH REALITIES
ROBERT VENDITTI writer DALE EAGLESHAM artist JASON WRIGHT colorist
cover art by BILLY TAN & ALEX SINCLAIR SCRIBBLENAUTS variant cover by JOHN KATZ after NEAL ADAMS

RELIC!

EASY, SAINT WALKER. YOU'VE BEEN UNCONSCIOUS FOR A *WHILE.*

BRAIN FUNCTIONS NORMAL. VITALS STEADY. I DON'T UNDERSTAND... HE'S MADE A *FULL* RECOVERY.

RELIC...

HE WAS IN GOOD HANDS, DOC.

I CAN'T TAKE CREDIT. THE HEALING PROPERTIES OF HIS *RING* MUST'VE DONE THE TRICK.

WARTH? W-WHERE IS BROTHER WARTH?

THE REST OF THE BLUE LANTERNS DIDN'T MAKE IT. *YOU* ARE THE LAST.

I'M SORRY.

THE BLUE LIGHT OF HOPE... *EXTINGUISHED.* WHAT MADNESS CAUSED THIS?

NOT JUST BLUE. RELIC CAME FOR US ALL. HE SAID OUR RINGS DRAIN THE EMOTIONAL ENERGY THAT FUELS THE UNIVERSE.

OR *SOMETHING.* ALL I KNOW IS IT LOOKS LIKE HE WAS RIGHT. KYLE STOPPED HIM AND SOME-HOW REFILLED THE RESERVOIR, BUT...

HE'S *GONE,* WALKER. KYLE DIED, TOO.

NO! EVERY BROTHER AND SISTER OF MY ORDER... *PERISHED.*

NOW...THIS. ALL THE JOURNEYS THE WHITE LANTERN AND I EMBARKED ON TOGETHER...

I SHOULD HAVE BEEN THERE TO *FIGHT* FOR HIM.

"...IF THERE'S ONE THING WE CAN'T AFFORD TO LOSE, IT'S HOPE."

THE COMMAND CENTER.

WHERE'S SINESTRO?

HE'S THE WILD CARD, KILOWOG.

WE NEED TO FIND WHERE HE AND HIS YELLOW LANTERNS ARE HOLED UP. HIT THEM WHILE THEY'RE IN DISARRAY.

WE TAKE DOWN THE SINESTRO CORPS, WE'LL HAVE DONE THE UNIVERSE A FAVOR.

WHAT ABOUT THE CONVICTS WE HAD TO TURN LOOSE WHEN OA WAS DESTROYED?

THOSE CROOKS ARE OUR RESPONSIBILITY, TOO.

CHANNELS OPEN.

CITIZENS OF THE UNIVERSE. FOR THOSE WHO DON'T RECOGNIZE ME, I'M *HAL JORDAN*, LEADER OF THE GREEN LANTERN CORPS.

THIS TRANSMISSION IS BEING BROADCAST FROM THE CORPS' HEADQUARTERS IN SECTOR ZERO.

THAT LEAVES *NO AMBIGUITY* ABOUT ITS AUTHENTICITY.

FOR BILLIONS OF YEARS, THE GREEN LANTERN CORPS HAS PROTECTED THE UNIVERSE FROM THREATS BOTH *PLANETARY* AND *INTERGALACTIC.*

TODAY, I CONFESS THAT WE'VE BEEN CONCEALING A *SECRET:* THERE'S A *NEW* THREAT FACING THE UNIVERSE, A THREAT THAT ENDANGERS *ALL* OF *CREATION.*

THAT THREAT--

--*IS* THE GREEN LANTERN CORPS.

IT WAS RECENTLY PROVEN THAT THE EMOTIONAL SPECTRUM CHANNELED THROUGH OUR RINGS ORIGINATES FROM A *RESERVOIR.*

WHAT--

THIS RESERVOIR CONTAINS A FINITE AMOUNT OF ENERGY. WHEN THAT ENERGY IS EXHAUSTED, THE UNIVERSE ENDS.

--THE *HELL*--

MOGO.

IF YOU THINK THAT MEANS THE GREEN LANTERN CORPS WILL CEASE USING THE MOST POWERFUL WEAPONS IN THE UNIVERSE--

--YOU'RE *WRONG.*

--IS THAT *POOZER*--

SPACE SECTOR 1416. THE PLANET ZAMARON.
HOME OF THE STAR SAPPHIRES.

WE'VE DEEMED THE DRAINING OF THE EMOTIONAL SPECTRUM TO BE A *NECESSARY* COST, WHETHER IT HARMS ALL OF YOU OR NOT.

WE WILL, HOWEVER, LESSEN THE COST BY TAKING DOWN *ANYONE* WHO WIELDS A RING AND ISN'T AN OFFICER OF THE CORPS.

--DOING?

RED ALERT PART 1
ROBERT VENDITTI writer BILLY TAN penciller ROB HUNTER inker ALEX SINCLAIR colorist
cover art by BILLY TAN & ALEX SINCLAIR

FASTER, BARREER. THERE'S *DISTANCE* TO COVER.

GRANTED. BUT WE SHOULD TAKE PAUSE, LOK. WE HAVE NO IDEA WHAT WE'RE FLYING INTO. COMMUNICATIONS ARE DOWN--

COMMS ARE DOWN BECAUSE THE CORPS IS UNDER *ASSAULT.*

I DON'T KNOW WHAT *YOU* HEARD BEFORE EVERYTHING WENT DARK, BUT *I* HEARD SECTOR HOUSES *BEGGING* FOR BACKUP.

LANTERNS ARE *UNDER SIEGE,* AND WE'RE ON THE OPPOSITE SIDE OF THE UNIVERSE!

UNFORTUNATELY, WE AREN'T ALONE. *LOOK.*

IF THAT'S WHAT I THINK IT IS--

WH OOOOM

AKK-GCL!

NNNGH

LOOK ALIVE ‹GRBT› BARREER!

SHIELD UP!

GNNGRRG!

KRA-KOOM

NNUHHGGH

MUST HAVE EXHAUSTED HERSELF.

NO WONDER. HAVE YOU EVER SEEN A BEING CHANNEL THE EMOTIONAL SPECTRUM THROUGH THEIR *EYES?*

I'VE NEVER EVEN *HEARD* OF THAT.

LET'S GET IT BACK TO H.Q. BEFORE IT COMES AROUND.

DIFFICULT NOT TO FEEL SOME MEASURE OF *PITY* FOR HER.

THE SPIT FROM ONE OF THOSE THINGS NEARLY *CORRODED* WARDEN VOZ'S *FACE* OFF.

HIM I FEEL BAD FOR.

THE ENLISTMENT OATH OF THE U.S. ARMED SERVICES? YOU *REALLY* THINK THAT MAKES ANYTHING OFFICIAL, HAL?

LIKE I SHOULD KNOW? I'VE NEVER SWORN IN *EX-CONVICTS*, JOHN.

THANKS FOR DROPPING THESE GUYS IN OUR LAPS, BY THE WAY.

ALL RIGHT, YOU'RE THE LAST GROUP!

ASSEMBLE WITH THE OTHERS FOR PROCEDURES BRIEFING AND MISSION ASSIGNMENTS!

ON THE QUICK, DEPUTIES!

PROCEDURES? ASSIGNMENTS? *BAH!*

YOU SHOULD BE HAPPY THEY DIDN'T SAY "DRESS CODE."

DID THINGS JUST GET BETTER FOR US, JOHN, OR *WORSE?*

THE KHUND AMBUSHED OUR SECTOR HOUSES. OL-ANJ'S BRAID CLANN *DYNAMITED* OUR COMMAND CENTER.

AND THE PHONY BROADCAST THAT DURLAN *SHAPE-SHIFTER* SENT OUT--THE ONE OF YOU GETTING YOUR *FASCIST* ON?--WILL MAKE ALLIES SCARCE.

NOW ISN'T THE TIME TO TURN AWAY ABLE BODIES WILLING TO FIGHT FOR US.

NO MATTER *WHERE* THEY COME FROM.

IT'S A *WRONG* DAY WHEN WE CAN COUNT ON *FELONS* OVER FELLOW LANTERNS, *EH,* GRAF?

MEANING *WHAT,* VATH? SPEAK YOUR MIND.

WHAT LITTLE THERE IS OF IT.

A DURLAN CAN TAKE THE SHAPE OF JUST ABOUT ANYTHING. UNIFORMS AND RINGS ARE A SNAP.

ONLY ONE WAY TO TELL A *REAL* LANTERN WEARING A REAL RING: SHED SOME *LIGHT.* BUT YOU'VE *CONVENIENTLY* SWORN OFF THAT, HAVEN'T YOU?

OUR RINGS DRAIN THE RESERVOIR OF THE EMOTIONAL SPECTRUM. I DON'T WIELD LIGHT ON *PRINCIPLE.*

SO YOU AND YOUR OBJECTORS SAY. OR MAYBE THAT'S JUST YOUR *COVER.*

ONE SPARK. GIMME JUST *ONE.*

IF YOU *CAN.*

WHUMP

AW, C'MON! SEE HOW *EASY* THAT WAS?

CURSE YOU, VATH.

THE DURLANS ARE RIGHT WHERE THEY WANT TO BE-- INSIDE OUR HEADS.

VATH HAS A POINT. ROUND UP THE CIVILIAN SUPPORT STAFF, VOZ.

NO WAY THE DURLANS COULD'VE SET UP SUCH A COORDINATED STRIKE UNLESS THEY HAD AGENTS KEEPING TABS ON US.

UNTIL WE KNOW FOR SURE WHO'S WHO, ANYONE WHO CAN'T USE A RING CAN'T BE TRUSTED AS FAR AS WE CAN--

RSSSTLE

RSSSTLE

...THROW THEM?

YEALLGH!

THE HELL?

≥WHUFF≤

LANTERNS! TO THE TREES!

MMRRGLU

GRRGMMR

WHAT IS THIS? *HOW* IS THIS?

WE ARRESTED HER IN SECTOR 3014.

IT DIDN'T COME QUIETLY.

BUT WHO IS SHE?

YOU GET KONKED ON THE HEAD OR SOMETHING? SHE'S A *RED.*

GRRGGLU.

THERE'S ONLY A HANDFUL OF REDS, KILOWOG. GUY, RANKORR, BLEEZ...THE BEACHBALL WITH THE STUMPY LIMBS. A COUPLE OTHERS.

THIS ONE I'VE NEVER SEEN. SHE'S *NEW.*

I DO **NOT** NEED THIS RIGHT NOW. BRINGING IN RECRUITS? WHAT ON **EARTH** IS GUY THINKING?

HE AIN'T **ON** EARTH ANYMORE.

JUST **ONE** CRISIS AT A TIME. IS THAT TOO MUCH TO ASK?

IT'S A BIG UNIVERSE. LOOK ON THE SUNNY SIDE. GUY BUILDING A BIGGER CORPS MEANS WE'VE GOT A BUNCH MORE POLICE WORK AHEAD OF US.

JOB SECURITY.

IF THERE ARE MORE OUT THERE LIKE THAT, YOU'LL WANT TO **RETIRE.**

IT'S SO JUICED UP, IT SHOT RED LIGHT FROM ITS EYES.

...DID YOU SAY **EYES?**

BLASTED AN ASTEROID TO GRAVEL.

RING, RUN SCAN. IDENTIFY.

SCAN COMPLETE.

SUBJECT IS KRYPTONIAN.

THAT'S...NOT POSSIBLE.

WHERE'S KRYPTONIA?

KRYPTON WAS IN SECTOR 2813, BUT IT ISN'T **ANY**-WHERE ANYMORE. IT **DIED.**

NOT MANY OF ITS PEOPLE SURVIVED. JUST **ONE,** AS FAR AS I KNOW.

SO THIS FEMALE IS SIGNIFICANT?

A KRYPTONIAN RED IS PRETTY MUCH THE **DEADLIEST** OF ALL POSSIBLE COMBINATIONS. THIS NEEDS TO BE DEALT WITH. **FAST.**

THEN LET'S DEAL WITH IT. HOLD HER DOWN WHILE I YANK HER RING OFF.

DON'T. THE TRANSFORMATION TO A RED LANTERN TAKES OVER THE VICTIM'S **HEART.** THE RING IS THE ONLY THING KEEPING HER **ALIVE** NOW.

POLICING THE USE OF THE EMOTIONAL SPECTRUM IS ONE THING, BUT I'M NOT GOING TO HAND OUT **DEATH** SENTENCES.

WHAT, THEN? STUFF HER IN A JAIL CELL? I DON'T MUCH LIKE THE SOUND OF THAT. THE OTHER INMATES WON'T, EITHER.

THAT'S WHY WE'RE GOING TO **CURE** HER.

THERE'S ONLY ONE THING IN THE UNIVERSE THAT CAN COMPLETELY REHABILITATE A RED LANTERN...

"...WE NEED THE BLUE LIGHT OF *HOPE*."

THANK YOU FOR SHOWING ME THIS PLACE, MOGO. ITS BEAUTY IS A SALVE FOR THE INJURED SOUL.

YOU ARE A WELCOME GUEST, SAINT WALKER. IT IS NOT OFTEN ONE SUCH AS MYSELF GETS TO SOCIALIZE WITH LESS PERMANENT LIFE FORMS.

A CELESTIAL EXISTENCE HAS ITS DISADVANTAGES.

AND A *LESS PERMANENT* ONE IS FILLED WITH REGRETS ONE HAS NOT THE TIME TO AMEND.

WALKER?

CAN WE TALK?

THAT'S WHERE YOU KEEP YOUR RING, MOGO? I ALWAYS ASSUMED IT WAS SOMEPLACE DOWN IN YOUR CORE.

SNFF SNFF

BUT THEN HOW WOULD THE TREEMUNKS PLAY WITH IT, CORPS LEADER JORDAN?

RIGHT... I GUESS THAT'S A GOOD POINT?

ANYWAY, CAN YOU LEAVE WALKER AND ME ALONE FOR A MINUTE?

I AM A PLANET. WHEREVER I GO, YOU WILL STILL BE HERE.

JUST FIND SOMETHING ELSE TO DO.

MAYBE YOU CAN TRACK DOWN THE DURLAN WHO COPIED ME? HE HAS TO BE HIDING *SOMEWHERE* ON-WORLD.

MY SURFACE IS A CACOPHONY OF LIFE.

IF I SOMETIMES SEEM...DISTRACTED, IT IS BECAUSE I CAN MONITOR THE CONSTANT ACTIVITIES OF MY INHABITANTS NO MORE EASILY THAN YOU CAN CATALOGUE THE MOVEMENTS OF BACTERIA ON YOUR SKIN.

DO NOT SEEK PRIVACY ON MY ACCOUNT, LANTERN JORDAN. WHEN IT COMES TO MOGO, I AM AN OPEN BOOK.

PLEASE. SIT.

TWO OF OUR LANTERNS PICKED UP A RED ON THEIR PATROL. A *KRYPTONIAN.* YOU HAVE TO REVERSE THE PROCESS BEFORE SHE *KILLS* SOMEONE.

I WOULD VERY MUCH LIKE TO AID YOU--

--BUT AS YOU CAN SEE, MY RING AND I ARE NOT ON SPEAKING TERMS AT THE MOMENT.

I UNDERSTAND HOW YOU FEEL.

NONE OF US ENJOYED HEARING THAT OUR RINGS ARE A DRAIN ON...PRETTY MUCH EVERYTHING. WHAT WAS IT RELIC CALLED US? "AGENTS OF DECAY."

BUT THE REST OF THE BLUE LANTERNS LAID DOWN THEIR LIVES SO *YOU* COULD GO ON. AND SO *HOPE* COULD STAY ALIVE WITH YOU.

I SAY THE UNIVERSE *NEEDS* LANTERNS LIKE US. GUYS WHO WIELD LIGHT FOR THE CAUSE OF GOOD. THAT'S WHY I'M NOT PUTTING DOWN MY RING.

NOT YET.

NOR WOULD I EXPECT YOU TO. WILLFULNESS IS THE PROVINCE OF GREEN LANTERNS. *YOU* MOST OF ALL.

WHEN CONFRONTED BY TRAGEDY, YOU SOLDIER ON UNDAUNTED. EVEN WHEN --INDEED, *ESPECIALLY* WHEN--THE TRAGEDY IS OF YOUR OWN MAKING.

I LOOK AT MY RING, AND I SEE ONLY THE HARM IT CAN CAUSE. HARM THAT CAN NO LONGER BE UNDONE.

THE GREEN LIGHT OF WILL *THRIVES* ON THE INSURMOUNTABLE. IT SHINES BRIGHTEST IN THE DARK. BUT TOO MUCH DARKNESS CASTS HOPE IN *SHADOW*.

THEN WE'LL BURN AWAY THE DARKNESS UNTIL NO SHADOWS REMAIN.

IF THE UNIVERSE *ENDURES*, IT'LL BE *BECAUSE* OF WHAT HOPE AND WILL DO TOGETHER. NOT IN SPITE OF IT.

I ADMIRE YOUR... RESOLVE. BUT DO NOT WASTE LIGHT ON MY ACCOUNT.

AS A FORMER DISCIPLE OF HOPE, HEAR ME: IT WOULD BE EASIER TO SIT MOGO ON YOUR KNEE THAN TO MAKE ANOTHER BEING *FEEL* SOMETHING IT DOES *NOT*.

IF HOPE IS TO BE FOUND AGAIN, LANTERN JORDAN, IT MUST BE *I* WHO FINDS IT.

UNTIL THEN, MY ROAD WILL BE TRAVELED ALONE.

"CAN YOU UNDERSTAND ME?"

"...BUT INSIDE, HE'LL ALWAYS BE GREEN."

SPACE SECTOR 2814.

THE PLANET YSMAULT. **HOME OF THE RED LANTERNS.**

WHERE ARE THE CRETINS?

YOUR GUESS IS AS GOOD AS MINE, IOLANDE.

I'VE NEVER BEEN HERE WHEN THEY WEREN'T STANDING AROUND THEIR BATTERY. IT'S KIND OF WHAT THEY DO.

BUT IT'S NICE TO SEE GUY'S NEW ROLE HASN'T CHANGED HIS TENDENCY TO OVER-COMPENSATE...

SUCH *PUTREFACTION.* NOTHING LIKE THE SEA OF GENERATIONS MY KIND RESIDES IN.

STRANGE...

...THEIR *SHIP* IS JUST SITTING OUT IN THE OPEN.

RED ALERT PART 2
CHARLES SOULE writer ALESSANDRO VITTI artist GABE ELTAEB colorist
cover art by STEPHEN SEGOVIA & HI-FI

SHIPPING OUT

ROBERT VENDITTI writer BILLY TAN & MARTIN COCCOLO pencillers ROB HUNTER & WALDEN WONG inkers
TONY AVIÑA & ALEX SINCLAIR colorists cover art by BILLY TAN & ALEX SINCLAIR ROBOT CHICKEN variant cover by RC STOODIOS

SPACE SECTOR 2814.
EARTH.
COAST CITY, CALIFORNIA.

KNOK KNOK

UNCLE HAL!

YOUR FOLKS LET YOU ANSWER THE DOOR NOW? GETTING TO BE A *BIG GUY,* HOWARD.

DAD! MOM! UNCLE HAL'S HERE!

LOOK WHO THE BREEZE BLEW IN!

I'LL SET YOU A PLACE FOR DINNER. YOUR BROTHER IS JUST ABOUT TO PUT IT ON THE TABLE.

UNCLE HAL!

THANKS, SUE. BUT I CAN'T STAY.

BULL. TIP-OFF IS IN A HALF HOUR. YOU CAN MAKE TIME FOR A GAME AND A BEER.

JIM...

...I CAN'T STAY.

WHAT'S GOING ON?

STAY, UNCLE HAL!

PLEEEASE!

I WISH I COULD, IDDOS. MORE THAN ANYTHING. BUT, SEE...UNCLE HAL SCREWED UP.

HE SCREWED UP A BUNCH OF THINGS, AND NOW HE HAS TO LEAVE FOR A WHILE.

ALREADY? ∻SNIFF∻ FOR HOW LONG?

I WISH I KNEW.

COME WITH ME, KIDS. LET DADDY AND UNCLE HAL TALK.

MOGO. **HURTLING THROUGH SPACE.**

THIS IS... *UNFATHOMABLE.* HAD YOU NOT SAID WE WERE IN TRANSIT, MOGO, I WOULD NEVER HAVE REALIZED.

CELESTIAL BODIES ARE IN CONSTANT MOTION, SAINT WALKER. THE ONLY DIFFERENCE IS I HAVE BROKEN ELLIPSE TO JOURNEY ON A STRAIGHT PATH.

"WHAT HAPPENS IF YOU REMAIN AWAY FROM YOUR SUN TOO LONG?"

"TO ME? NOTHING. HOWEVER, MY SURFACE WILL BECOME QUITE... INHOSPITABLE TO ITS MANY LIFE FORMS.

"DO NOT BE CONCERNED, MY FRIEND. THERE WILL BE A NEW SUN FOR US TO BASK IN, AFTER WE HAVE PASSED THROUGH THE LONG NIGHT."

YOU MAKE IT SOUND A TRIVIAL THING. *RELOCATING* TO A *WAR ZONE.*

CORPS LEADER JORDAN BELIEVES WE WILL BE BETTER ABLE TO QUELL THE UPRISING IF WE ARE POSITIONED CLOSE TO THE COMBAT.

THE STRATEGY IS NOT WITHOUT MERIT. DO YOU NOT AGREE?

AS FIRST OF THE BLUE LANTERNS, I WAS A CHAMPION OF *HOPE* AND *PEACE.* WAR HAS NEVER BEEN MY SPECIALTY.

I STILL HAVE NO STOMACH FOR IT. EVEN NOW THAT I HAVE LOST MY...ABILITY TO WEAR A RING.

WHAT OF YOU? WHAT CONCERN OF YOURS ARE THE QUARRELS OF US LESSER BEINGS?

CIVILIZATIONS MUST BE GOVERNED, OR THEY WILL HARM EVERYTHING AROUND THEM.

A SOLITARY EXISTENCE HAS NOT PREVENTED ME FROM UNDERSTANDING THIS TRUTH.

THE CORPS' MISSION IS NOBLE IN CONCEPT, IF NOT ALWAYS EXECUTION. BUT FAILURE IS THE FERTILE SOIL OF SUCCESS. IN TIME, THE JUST WILL PREVAIL.

"ALL WILL BE WELL"? I HAVE SEEN TOO MUCH TO SHARE YOUR OPTIMISM.

WITHOUT OPTIMISM, WE MAY AS WELL ALL GO BACK TO SLEEP.

EVERY LANTERN I SHEPHERDED... I TAUGHT THEM TO WIELD THE LIGHT, AND UNKNOWINGLY MADE THEM DETRIMENTS TO CREATION.

BROTHER WARTH, SISTER SERCY, *LANTERN RAYNER*...THEY ALL LOST THEIR LIVES BECAUSE OF ME.

THERE IS HOPE WITHIN YOU YET, SAINT WALKER, EVEN IF YOU DO NOT ACKNOWLEDGE IT.

I AM A SAINT NO MORE.

I AM ONLY A WALKER.

WISHFUL THINKING, EH, SALAAK...?

HOPING ALL RELIC'S *LIGHT-DRAINING* TECH GOT DESTROYED WITH HIM.

WE KNOW AT LEAST ONE *DURLAN* CONCEALED ITSELF AMONG THE SUPPORT STAFF I EVACUATED FROM OA...

DIRTY *SHAPE-SHIFTER* COULDA LAID TENTACLES ON A DRAINER, EASY.

WHO DO YOU FIGURE DID THE MODS TO THIS ONE? WE FOUND IT IN A SECTOR HOUSE ATTACKED BY THE *KHUND*, BUT THIS AIN'T THEIR WORK.

KZZZ

TRUE. THIS VERSION IS MORE...*REFINED* THAN RELIC'S ITERATION.

TOO REFINED FOR THE *BLUNT* HANDS OF THE KHUND. THE WORK WAS OUTSOURCED. BUT TO WHOM?

I HAVE AN IDEA.

WHAT'S THE STATUS REPORT?

SYSTEMS ARE BACK UP AND RUNNING. TOOK SOME CREATIVE ENGINEERING, BUT THEY'LL HOLD.

BZZZT

THEY'LL HOLD?

THMP THMP

ZZZT

NOW THEY'LL HOLD.

AND WHAT ABOUT THE DURLAN WHO HELPED PLANT THE BOMB? ANY LUCK FINDING IT?

NOT YET. HOWEVER, THE REST OF THE SUPPORT STAFF HAS BEEN PUT ON LEAVE AS A PRECAUTION. NO ONE ABSENT A *WORKING* RING IS PERMITTED ON THE GROUNDS.

YOU ASKED TO SEE ME, CORPS LEADER?

NOT *JUST* YOU, TWO-SIX.

I WANT TO TALK TO *ALL* OF YOU. TAKE A SEAT.

THAT'S RIGHT, I'M THINKING *AHEAD.* NO ONE IS MORE SHOCKED THAN ME.

SO, HOW ABOUT IT?

I ACCEPT.

YOU HAD ME AT "ANALYTICAL."

YOU KNOW YOU DON'T GOTTA ASK, PAL.

ALL RIGHT. LANTERN KHO LEANED ON HER CONTACTS INSIDE THE KHUND MILITARY. SHE HEARD *GWOTTLE* IS WHERE THE HACKED-OUT LIGHT DRAINERS ARE BEING BUILT.

WHAT'S OUR MOVE?

THE HOUSES WE LOST IN THE COORDINATED STRIKE ARE SCATTERED ACROSS *DOZENS* OF SECTORS.

EVEN WITH THEIR DURLAN AND OUTER CLANN ALLIES, THE KHUND STILL LACK THE FORCES NECESSARY TO PATROL A TERRITORY SO LARGE.

THEY'LL EXPECT US TO HIT 'EM AT THE EDGES, BUT I SAY WE POSITION MOGO *DEAD CENTER.*

SEE HOW *THEY* LIKE BEING INVADED. BESIDES, WE POKE OUR FINGER IN THEIR EYE, THEY'LL BE LESS LIKELY TO SET THEIR SIGHTS ON *CIVILIAN* WORLDS.

AND IF GWOTTLE IS THE SPOT, OUR FIRST MOVE IS TO BREAK THE SUPPLY CHAIN. CAN'T HAVE THE ENEMY ARMING THEMSELVES WITH *ANTI-LIGHT* TECH.

I LIKE IT. KILOWOG, PUT TOGETHER A TEAM. SALAAK, BRIEF THEM ON GWOTTLE.

AS SOON AS MOGO DROPS ANCHOR, I'M GOING IN.

DON'T SUPPOSE YOU'D LEAD FROM H.Q., AND LET THE *TROOPS* DO THE FIGHTING?

BABY STEPS, KILOWOG.

LET'S GET TO IT, LANTERNS.

WE'VE GOT GROUND TO MAKE UP.

GWOTTLE POPULATION: 453 MILLION

SPACE SECTOR 0487.

THE PLANET GWOTTLE. INTERSTELLAR INDUSTRIAL CENTER.

LOAD THE DEVICES FOR TRANSPORT!

WWWMMMMMMMMMZZZZZZ

WMMMMMZZ

HHHNNNNNN

GAH!

RAARGH!

HOW'RE THEY →NNG← *CONTROLLING* THESE THINGS?

FOUND THE *REMOTE*, HAL!

USE YOUR RING TO CRACK THE ENCRYPTION! *HURRY!*

NOT ENOUGH *TIME.*

SSSZZZTTTTT

GORIN-SUNN! WHAT'RE YOU DOING?!

ZZRT

ZZRT

ZZRT

THE GWOTTLENS MAKE A BAD BATCH?

I'M *LIVING ENERGY*, HAL. INTERFACING WITH ELECTRONICS ISN'T REALLY A PROBLEM.

YOU HAVE *NO IDEA* OF THE FORCES GATHERED AGAINST YOU, LANTERNS. GWOTTLE IS BUT *ONE* OF THE *MANY* WORLDS WHO'VE JOINED OUR FIGHT.

GWOTTLENS ARE FRIENDS OF THE CORPS. YOU'RE *BUILDERS*, NOT *WARMONGERS.* WHY DO THIS?

WE DON'T SIX-SHAKE WITH TYRANTS.

YOUR RINGS DRAIN THE LIFE-LIGHT OF THE UNIVERSE. AS LONG AS YOU CONTINUE TO USE THEM, GWOTTLE WILL STAND AGAINST YOU.

HAL? WHAT ARE YOUR *ORDERS?*

YOU'RE ON PRISONER DETAIL, VODE-M.

VATH, ESCORT THE GWOTTLENS OUT OF THE FACTORY.

MAKE SURE THE BUILDING IS CLEAR. LET THEM GO, AND THEN YOU AND BARREER *LEVEL* THE COMPLEX.

WHAT? THESE TINKERERS SUPPLIED AMMO TO THE *ENEMY!*

WANT TO ARREST THE ENTIRE PLANET? THEN WE *WILL* BE TYRANTS. THE GWOTTLENS ARE *PAWNS.*

BESIDES, I'M *SAVING* MY ANGER--

WE NOTCHED A WIN TODAY, BUT WHAT GOOD IS THAT IF OUR REPUTATION COMES THROUGH IN TATTERS?

WINNING FISTFIGHTS ISN'T GOING TO BE ENOUGH THIS TIME.

WE HAVE TO WIN HEARTS AND MINDS.

DEATH AND LIFE
ROBERT VENDITTI writer MARTIN COCCOLO artist TONY AVIÑA & ALEX SINCLAIR colorists
cover art by BILLY TAN & ALEX SINCLAIR MAD variant cover by RICHARD WILLIAMS

SPACE SECTOR 0440.
THE SENTIENT PLANET MOGO. MOBILE HEADQUARTERS OF THE INTERGALACTIC POLICE FORCE KNOWN AS THE GREEN LANTERN CORPS.

BEAUTIFUL...

I WAS THINKING "PEACEFUL." HASN'T BEEN MUCH OF THAT LATELY, MORRO.

MY HOMEWORLD IS A CEASELESS DESERT. WALKING THE SANDS, I NEVER KNEW THERE EXISTED SUCH A THING AS THE COLOR *GREEN.*

MY BROTHER, MARRG--REST HIS SOLES-- WOULD NEVER COMPREHEND WHERE BEING A LANTERN HAS TAKEN ME...

THEY'RE *GATHERED,* HAL. IT'S *TIME.*

DID YOU HAVE TO FINISH SO QUICKLY? THIS IS *ONE* JOB I'D LIKE TO KEEP PUTTING OFF FOR ANOTHER DAY...

I SUSPECT LANTERN STEWART FEELS THE SAME. ELSE HE WOULD'VE DONE THE CONSTRUCTING FOR ME WHEN HE DESIGNED OUR NEW HOME.

IT'S DIFFICULT FOR SOME TO ACCEPT THAT THE SOUL OF THE CORPS ISN'T THE CITADEL OR THE MESS HALL.

IT ISN'T THE BARRACKS AND ITS 7200 LOCKERS FILLED WITH MEMORIES FROM EACH LANTERN'S HOME.

THE SOUL OF THE CORPS IS TH PLACE WHERE *EVE* LANTERN'S JOURN WILL ONE DAY EN

WE'RE AT *WAR.* WE'VE LOST OUR STANDING IN THE UNIVERSE...WITH GOOD REASON. THE OLD GUARDIANS TURNED OUT TO BE WAY MORE *EVIL* THAN THE THREATS THEY CLAIMED TO OPPOSE.

BUT THIS IS *MY* FAULT, TOO. I HAVEN'T *LED* AS I SHOULD'VE. AND *THAT* IS GOING TO CHANGE.

THIS ISN'T A WAR FOR TERRITORY. IT'S A WAR FOR THE *FUTURE* OF THE UNIVERSE ITSELF.

THERE'S WORK TO DO. BUT IF WE HOLD OURSELVES TO KYLE'S STANDARD, THE UNIVERSE WILL REMEMBER WHY IT BELIEVED IN US--AND WILL *AGAIN.*

AND THEN WE'LL HAVE EARNED THE *PRIVILEGE* TO WEAR OUR RINGS.

BURN BRIGHT, KYLE RAYNER.

BURN BRIGHT!

NOT ONE DROP OF RAIN FALLS ON THIS PLACE, MOGO.

I WILL MONITOR MY WEATHER PATTERNS, CORPS LEADER. YOU HAVE MY PROMISE.

GOOD WORDS.

I'D BE HAPPIER NOT SAYING THEM, KILOWOG.

AND I WISH I COULD'VE REACHED *CAROL*. I HAVEN'T TALKED TO HER SINCE...

WELL, I JUST KNOW THIS HAS TO BE HARD ON HER, TOO.

MORRO DID RIGHT WITH THE PLACE. STILL, I *NEVER* WANT TO SET FOOT INSIDE HERE AGAIN.

IT'S MY JOB TO MAKE SURE NO OTHER LANTERN DOES, EITHER.

YOUR JOB IS TO *WIN* THE *WAR*, LANTERN JORDAN.

WHAT SALAAK SAID.

WEARING THE UNIFORM AIN'T A SAFE PLAY FOR ANY OF US. WE KNEW THAT THE FIRST TIME A RING LANDED ON OUR FINGER.

KYLE NEVER FORGOT IT. *NONE* OF US HAVE.

IF THERE *IS* A PLANE AFTER THIS EXISTENCE, I CAN STAND VERTICAL THERE KNOWING MORRO RAISED A STONE FOR ME HERE.

DARN TOOTIN', TWO-SIX.

WHEN MY TIME COMES, SAY A FEW WORDS OVER ME?

A FEW? I CAN MANAGE THAT.

"WE MUST *MEET* WITH THE EMISSARY."

SALAAK! YOU OLD *SOUR FACE!*

THAT'S THE *BIG MAN* 'ROUND HERE?

SHHH.

IT HAS BEEN TOO LONG, EMISSARY PREEGUS.

THANKS FOR BRINGING YOUR BOSS.

TERRIBLE THING, THIS CONFLICT. I'VE BEEN SHOULDERED WITH MAKING SURE THE *NEUTRALITY* OF OASIS BAY, AND THE REST OF EBBEN TRADING COMPANY'S HOLDINGS, IS RESPECTED--

LANTERN *MAGGOTS.*

YOUR *AIM* AS SHARP AS YOUR *WORDS,* KHUND?

DO NOT! E.T.C. PORTS ARE *NEUTRAL* GROUND!

OUTTA THE WAY, *GNAT!*

CAPTAIN KHU, LOWER YOUR GUNS.

I ASKED YOU *AND* THE LANTERNS TO THIS SIT-DOWN TO REASSERT OUR POSITION OF *UNINVOLVEMENT* IN THIS CONFLICT.

THEY *AMBUSHED* OUR SECTOR HOUSES! WE LOST GOOD PEOPLE!

THOSE WERE YOUR *GOOD* LANTERNS? HOW POORLY DO YOUR *BAD* ONES FIGHT?

PREEGUS, ARE YOU *ADDLED?*

NEUTRALITY IS OUR *FOUNDING PRINCIPLE.* THE CORPS' CONFLICTS ARE NOT OUR CONCERN. WE SIGNED A TREATY WITH YOUR GUARDIANS STATING SUCH. IT'S LASTED GENERATIONS.

DOES THE CORPS NO LONGER *HONOR* ITS AGREEMENTS?

YOU'RE *HARBORING* THE *KHUND WAR MACHINE!*

AND WE'LL HARBOR *YOU,* IF YOU EVER NEED IT. NO MATTER WHAT. IT'S OUR WAY.

UNLESS YOU BREAK OUR TREATY TODAY. THEN YOU WILL COUNT E.T.C.-- AND ITS *CONSIDERABLE* SUPPORT AND RESUPPLY ASSETS--AMONG YOUR OPPOSITION.

THE *VAUNTED* LANTERNS. LOOK HOW THE TINY EMISSARY STAYS THEM.

"--OASIS BAY'S *AMENITIES* ARE AT YOUR DISPOSAL."

I APOLOGIZE, LANTERN JORDAN. I SHOULD HAVE BRIEFED YOU ON LOCAL CUSTOMS.

DON'T BEAT YOURSELF UP, SALAAK. AN ENTIRE BATTLE DECIDED BETWEEN TWO MEN IN A ROOM? IF ONLY *ALL* WARS COULD BE FOUGHT THIS WAY.

BESIDES, WEARING THE UNIFORM ISN'T A SAFE PLAY FOR ANY OF US, RIGHT?

ESTIMATING MASS AND ACCELERATION, I CALCULATE IT WILL BE DIFFICULT FOR YOU TO COUNTER THE FORCE OF CAPTAIN KHU'S ATTACK.

IT AIN'T ALWAYS ABOUT THE MATH, TWO-SIX.

NOBODY BEATS DEATH LIKE JORDAN. AND A *KNIFE FIGHT* WITH A *KHUND? THAT'S* DEATH.

I'LL DRINK TO THAT. NOTHING LIKE A LITTLE *LIQUID COURAGE.*

WELL SAID.

I'M PLEASED OUR REPUTATION ISN'T LOST ON YOU.

PULL UP A CHAIR, KHU. I'M BUYING.

YOU *DARE* SPEAK TO--

CRIPES. YOU MUST BE *NEW.* ANY VET KNOWS TO MAKE THE *MOST* OF HIS LEAVE, NO MATTER *WHO* HE SHARES THE BAR WITH.

HAVE A DRINK, SPARKY. IT'LL MELLOW YOU OUT.

"MAY THE BEST MAN WIN."

UHNN

SOMETIMES IT *IS* ABOUT THE MATH.

JORDAN!

GET UP!

FORFEIT, LANTERN.

WHUMP

I'LL TAKE *YOUR* HEAD--

KRAKK

--BUT SPARE THE *OTHERS* THE SAME FATE.

A TRIBUTE TO YOUR *WARRIOR* SPIRIT.

QUIT? I'M A LITTLE :NNN: *HARDHEADED* FOR THAT.

A *WARRIOR* TO THE END.

AS YOU WILL IT.

WILL.

CHAK

GOOD WORD.

KKARRUNCH

YOU'RE ALWAYS *CHARGING*, KHU.

TAKE IT FROM *ME*. PUSH *FORWARD* TOO HARD--

GYALUK!

SSKKLITCH

--YOU END UP WITH YOUR *BACK* AGAINST A *WALL*.

...

CAPTAIN!

≈HUFF≈

≈HUFF≈

THWUMP

--I CAN'T LET YOU LIVE.

FWASSH

WARDEN VOZ! I FOUND THE *DURLAN!*

SLUURRRKK

CRYING OUT *LOUD,* MUKMUK! WE'RE SUPPOSED TO *CAPTURE* HIM. HOW WE GOING TO FIND OUT IF THERE ARE *MORE* HIDING ON MOGO?

IT CHANGED INTO A CALTOOSIAN *SEA DRAGON!* WHA WAS I SUPPOSED TO DO?

:HMPH: WELL, *YOU'RE* LUGGING THAT THING BACK TO H.Q.

HAL WILL BE GLAD THE *DIRTY SPY* FINALLY PAID FOR ITS CRIME.

UPRISING PART 1: BATTLE OF WILLS

ROBERT VENDITTI writer BILLY TAN penciller ROB HUNTER inker ALEX SINCLAIR colorist
cover art by BILLY TAN & ALEX SINCLAIR BATMAN '66 variant cover by MIKE & LAURA ALLRED

AS WILL THE DURLANS.

...I DIDN'T KNOW THOSE OF YOUR RANK EVER LEFT DURLA, ANCIENT.

NOT IN **GENERATIONS.** BUT THE ANCIENTS BROUGHT THE KHUND AND THE OUTER CLANNS TOGETHER TO FORM THIS UPRISING.

A DAY SUCH AS **THIS** SHOULD BE WITNESSED BY A DURLAN LORD.

OUR PEOPLES HAVE SUFFERED UNDER THE RULE OF LANTERN LAW. OUR WORLDS, OUR WAY OF LIFE...EVEN OUR **BODIES,** DEFORMED.

IT IS TIME FOR THE AGE OF THE **GREEN LANTERNS** TO END.

WE HAVE INFLICTED MANY **CUTS.** THE LANTERNS' SECTOR HOUSES, DESTROYED. THEIR RANKS, DEPLETED. THEIR CONFIDENCE, BROKEN.

WORLDS WHERE THEY WERE ONCE WELCOME NOW JOIN US IN **CHALLENGING** THEM.

THEY THINK THEMSELVES SAFE ON THEIR NEW HOMEWORLD? WE WILL SHOW THEM THAT THEY HAVE **NO** HAVENS LEFT.

NO MORE **CUTS.** OUR AGENTS ARE WAITING.

YOU WON'T USE YOUR RINGS BECAUSE YOU'RE CONSERVING LIGHT, RIGHT? THEN I CAN'T PUT YOU ON THE FRONT LINE. YOU'LL BE SITTING DUCKS.

SO YOU MAKE US *MECHANICS?* MY FATHER *DIED* FOR THIS CORPS. I RATE BETTER.

ANY OF US DOES.

YOU'RE A VETERAN LANTERN, TOMAR-TU. SMART. *EXPERIENCED.*

FIGURE OUT THE KHUND NAVY'S STRENGTHS. FIND ITS SOFT SPOTS. LEARN HOW THEY CAN *KILL* US, AND HOW WE CAN MAKE THEM *NOT* KILL US.

BRING ME INTEL, AND WE'LL WIN THE NEXT BATTLE *BEFORE* IT'S FOUGHT.

INTEL. WE CAN DO THAT.

YOU'VE GAINED A FEW MORE FOLLOWERS.

THE DURLANS *FAKED* YOUR DECLARATION TO THE UNIVERSE, BUT THAT DOESN'T MAKE THE WORDS OF THE ANNOUNCEMENT ANY LESS TRUE.

THERE *IS* A RESERVOIR OF THE EMOTIONAL SPECTRUM. OUR RINGS *DO* DRAIN IT AT A COST TO CREATION. THE RULES FOR WIELDING LIGHT HAVE *CHANGED,* HAL. EACH OF US MUST RECONCILE WITH THAT IN OUR OWN WAY.

JUST MAKE SURE THEY UNDERSTAND THE *DROKKUN* INSIDE AND OUT.

BECAUSE THEY'RE GOING TO HELP YOU *FLY* IT.

NOW WE'RE TALKING.

WHAT'S ON THE MENU, GORIN-SUNN?

THERE ISN'T ONE POSTED, KILOWOG.

THE KITCHEN STAFF *DID* TURN OUT TO BE SHAPE-SHIFTERS IN DISGUISE...

A BIT OF HUNGER IS A SMALL SACRIFICE FOR KNOWING OUR DURLAN INFESTATION HAS BEEN ERADICATED.

SMALL FOR *YOU*, MAYBE.

EH, I'M JUST HERE FOR THE CONVERSATION. NOTHING OPENS A LANTERN'S MOUTH LIKE FOOD.

YOU... DON'T EAT?

I'M *LIVING ENERGY*. I DON'T NEED SUSTENANCE.

MY PEOPLE JUST SORT OF...MAINTAIN.

I VISITED YOUR WORLD ONCE. IT IS AN IMPRESSIVE SIGHT, THE LAKE YOU COME FROM.

YOU MEAN THE *SEA* OF GENERATIONS.

TELL *THAT* TO GRAF AND HIS OBJECTORS.

"*ALL* LIFE ON ZEZZEN IS IN THE SEA. NOT MUCH CHOICE. WE CAN'T STAY SEPARATED FROM IT AND LIVE.

"I'M THE FIRST ZEZZITE TO *EVER* JOURNEY *OFF-WORLD*, THANKS TO MY RING AND THIS *CONTAINMENT CONSTRUCT*."

GLAD YOU'RE ALL HERE.

ANY LUCK ON MAKING A *DURLAN DETECTOR*, SALAAK?

IT IS A DIFFICULT TASK. DURLANS COPY A SUBJECT DOWN TO ITS *DNA.* THE PROCESS RENDERS OUR RINGS' TRADITIONAL IDENT SCANS MOOT.

KEEP AT IT.

IN THE MEANTIME, TWO-SIX, POLL THE RECRUITS AND FIND GOOD FITS FOR SUPPORT STAFF. INFIRMARY IS AT THE TOP OF THE LIST.

I SPEAK FOR ALL RECRUITS WHEN I SAY WE DESIRE TO *FIGHT*, LIKE ANY LANTERN...

I RESPECT THAT. I DO. BUT WE'RE AT WAR, AND WITH SORANIK *M.I.A.*, WE DON'T EVEN HAVE A *CHIEF MEDICAL OFFICER.*

OR A *COOK*--AND A MILITARY MOVES ON ITS DIGESTIVE SAC.

THAT'S...GROSSER THAN HOW WE SAY IT ON EARTH, BUT YEAH.

I UNDER-STAND.

WE NEED AN *ATTACK PLAN*, TOO. AFTER THE *DROKKUN* GIVES UP ITS SECRETS, WE'RE GOING AFTER THE KHUND NAVY.

I'LL GET STARTED.

I APOLOGIZE FOR INTERRUPTING, CORPS LEADER JORDAN.

GO AHEAD, MOGO.

I BELIEVE THERE MAY BE UNIDENTIFIED SPACECRAFT ENTERING OUR CURRENT STAR SYSTEM...

KILOWOG! GET TO THE COMMAND CENTER!

EVERYONE! SCRAMBLE AND HOLD ON MY POSITION!

I DON'T WANT TO BELIEVE IT...

JORDAN, THEY AIN'T *JUST* KHUND SHIPS.

GWOTTLEN, NEWELLIAN, BROXITE CRUISERS...

"THESE ARE OUR *FRIENDS.*"

JRUK RECOGNIZES A VESSEL OF HIS PLANET.

I SEE ONE FROM *MY* WORLD, TOO...

RING! TRANSMIT TO THOSE SHIPS!

HE ORANXIAN BATTLESHIP NARONX.

PEOPLE OF THE UNIVERSE... YOU'RE BEING *MISLED.*

THE GREEN LANTERN CORPS ISN'T PERFECT, BUT WE'RE *STILL* YOUR PROTECTORS.

PLEASE. DON'T DO THIS. REMEMBER ALL THE *GOOD* WE'VE DONE IN THE UNIVERSE.

THINK OF THE GOOD WE CAN *STILL* DO.

THE NUMERICRON BASE CRUISER 3154.

A DURLAN IS *EVERYTHING*.

THAT WAS *LANTERN* ENERGY!

EVERYONE *HOLD FIRE*, DAMMIT!

NO!

A DURLAN IS *EVERYTHING!*

A DURLAN IS *EVERYWHERE!*

OH, *GOD*...

GENERAL, YOU HAVE YOUR *SIGNAL*.

FLEET! DO YOU *SEE?* THE LANTERNS SAY THEY WIELD LIGHT TO PRESERVE *LIFE*, BUT THEY PRACTICE *DEATH!*

THERE'LL BE NO *TRUCE* TODAY!

"*ATTACK!*"

ZZZAK

ZZZAK

BRAKOOM

CHOOM

CHOOM

BRAKOOM!

ZZZAK

PRESS THE ATTACK! *FINISH* THEM!

NO. OUR AGENTS HAVE BEEN *REVEALED.* THE ELEMENT OF SURPRISE HAS BEEN LOST. THE FLEET *CANNOT* SURVIVE AGAINST SO MANY LANTERNS.

ORDER THE RETREAT.

YOUR *IMPOSTORS* DIED BEFORE THEY COULD DO ANY *REAL* DAMAGE. YOUR STRATEGY *FAILS* AND YOU *FLEE?*

IT'S TIME FOR *KHUNDISH* MIGHT.

E BA
STI
R

THE IMPOSTORS-- AND THE CONFUSION THEY SOWED--*WERE* THE BATTLE. WITHOUT THEM, THE *PLANET* LANTERN WILL NOW BE IN PLAY.

WE CANNOT ST ND AGAINST I

A DURLAN ALWAYS HAS MORE THAN ONE STRATAGEM. THERE ARE MANY WAYS TO WIELD A DAGGER, AND MANY WOUNDS THAT KILL.

UPRISING PART 2: PRISON BREAK
VAN JENSEN writer BERNARD CHANG artist MARCELO MAIOLO colorist
cover art by STEPHEN SEGOVIA & ANDREW DALHOUSE BATMAN '66 variant cover by MIKE & LAURA ALLRED

"YOU MUST ACT QUICKLY. **KILL** THE PRISONERS--"

--KILL THEM NOW.

THERE IS STILL INFORMATION WE CAN *EXTRACT* FROM THE LANTERNS. I THINK THIS A WASTE--

WE DID NOT RECRUIT THE KHUND TO **THINK**. YOU HAVE YOUR ORDERS-- NOW **EXECUTE** THEM.

YOU DURLANS BOAST *DAILY* OF YOUR PATIENCE IN DESTROYING THE CORPS. WHAT HAS HAPPENED TO YOUR GRAND SCHEMES?

WE HAVE NO **TIME** FOR PATIENCE. THE ATTACK ON MOGO FAILED.

OUR LANTERN INFILTRATORS HAVE FALLEN. EVEN NOW, THE RINGS SEEK THEIR **TRUE** OWNERS.

...NO.

DOWN TO THE CELLS!

HURRY!

JOHN STEWART	FATALITY	JRUK	FESKA	PENELOPS	ARISIA	GHR'LL	XYLPTH	TURYTT	BLOOD COE

WHAT IS IT YOU PROPOSE, XYLPTH? WE HAVE NO RINGS.

THE *RING* DOES NOT MAKE THE LANTERN! YOU FORGET HOW *STRONG* YOUR HEART IS.

I SAY WE *FIGHT.* I SAY WE SHOW THEM WHAT MAKES ONE WORTHY OF THE CORPS--

I SAY YOU'RE ABOUT TO GET YOUR *CHANCE...*

"...THERE'S COMPANY NEXT DOOR."

ON YOUR FEET, LANTERN!

NO, DON'T--

KZZZAP

AAAIIIEEE--

LET ME *AT* THEM!

WATCH OUT, TURYTT!

THANKS. NOW GET THE HELL BACK. THOSE KHUND--

--ARE *DEAD*.

YOU'LL HAVE PLENTY TO FIGHT...

...FIRST, FREE THE OTHERS. WE NEED MORE--

UHN--!

HRM?

HM?

KBOOOM

WE CARVED A PATH THROUGH THE PRISON--WE'LL FOLLOW THAT BACK TO THE SURFACE. THOSE WHO STILL HAVE POWER, CARRY THOSE WHO DON'T.

WE CAN'T LEAVE. NOT YET.

I WANT TO MAKE THEM PAY AS MUCH AS YOU DO, XYLPTH. BUT THEY HAVE AN ARMY, AND WE DON'T.

THAT'S NOT WHAT I'M SAYING--THIS ISN'T EVERYONE. THE GUARDS MENTIONED ANOTHER PRISONER, EVEN FARTHER BELOW.

IT SOUNDS LIKE THEY TORTURED HIM, PUT HIM THROUGH EVEN WORSE THAN US. WHOEVER IT IS, HE'S BEEN HERE LONGER THAN THE REST OF US.

IT MIGHT NOT BE A LANTERN...

...BUT NO ONE DESERVES TO DIE HERE.

LET THE **KHUND** SUFFER THE BRUNT OF THE LANTERNS' ANGER.

FOR THEIR **MISTAKES**, THEY **DESERVE** IT.

WE CANNOT TAKE HALF MEASURES. THE LANTERNS MUST NOT ESCAPE--EVEN IF IT COSTS US THE **LAST** OF OUR SUSTENANCE.

CONSUME IT **ALL**.

YOU KNOW WHAT FORMS TO TAKE.

SLURRRK

THE FARTHER DOWN YOU GO, THE DEEPER YOU DIG YOUR GRAVES.

WE DISCOVERED AND REPLICATED THIS SPECIES RECENTLY.

JRUK-- NO!

HOW DEEP DOES THIS THING GO?

GRAALGH

THE WALLS ARE THICKER HERE. THE GUARDS ARE THINNING OUT. I'D SAY WE'RE CLOSE TO THE BOTTOM.

THEY HAVE QUITE THE APPETITE--

--BUT THEY CAN'T KEEP ANYTHING DOWN.

DON'T WASTE YOUR RING ENERGY ON THEM.

THEY'LL JUST TURN IT BACK AGAINST US.

WE KEEP GOING DOWN.

THIS HAS TO BE IT.

RING: RUN AN ANALYSIS. HOW DO WE FORCE IT OPEN?

STRUCTURE IS SOLID INERTRON WITH LEAD COATING. NO APPARENT STRUCTURAL WEAKNESSES.

LET ME.

THIS ISN'T DECORATIVE-- IT'S THE LOCK. I THINK I CAN TRIGGER IT.

HOW DO YOU--?

BEFORE I WAS A LANTERN... I WAS A THIEF.

I... ALMOST... HAVE...

...IT--

NO! DO NOT RELEASE--

REEEEE--!

SKKKKK

WHAT THE HELL--?

I THOUGHT...THE CORPS...FORGOT ABOUT ME...

BRRRMM

THE DURLANS... CAPTURED ME...

THEY EXPERIMENTED... ON ME...TRIED TO COPY MY FORM. THEY LEARNED HOW...TO REMOVE...MY RING.

WE KNOW. THE DURLANS BUILT A TEAM OF *LANTERN IMPOSTORS*. BUT WE BEAT THEM. WE HAVE MOST OF THE RINGS--WE'LL FIND YOURS, TOO. DON'T WORRY, THE CORPS IS SAFE.

BUT THEY... NEVER INTERROGATED ME...ABOUT THE CORPS. THEY ONLY WANTED TO KNOW...ABOUT MY *HOME* PLANET.

THE DURLANS HAD NEVER...HEARD OF...A DAXAMITE... UNTIL THEY FOUND ME.

MY GOD... *THAT'S* WHAT THEY WERE AFTER ALL ALONG.

MOGO WASN'T THE *REAL* TARGET--

--THE DURLANS ARE GOING TO INVADE *DAXAM!* WITH THAT *DNA*, THEY'LL BUILD AN *ARMY* OF SUPER-MEN.

IF THEY SUCCEED-- THE CORPS WON'T STAND A *CHANCE.*

UPRISING PART 3: SEA CHANGE
ROBERT VENDITTI writer BILLY TAN penciller ROB HUNTER & JAIME MENDOZA inkers TONY AVIÑA colorist
cover art by BILLY TAN & ALEX SINCLAIR BOMBSHELL variant cover by J.G JONES & ALEX SINCLAIR

PRIXIAM?

WE'VE BEEN *BACK-KNIFED,* CLANNERS! TO THE *STARCUTTER!*

NOW!

DID SOMETHING TRIGGER A CHAIN REACTION?

RING, REPLAY THE LAST THIRTY SECONDS OF DATA. IDENTIFY THE CAUSE OF THE EXPLOSIONS.

REMOTE SIGNAL DETECTED. SOURCE UNKNOWN.

NO SURIVORS, HAL. THE ENTIRE GARRISON IS *LIMBS* AND *RUBBLE*.

I'VE HEARD OF THE KHUND GOING *KAMIKAZE*, BUT THIS DOESN'T LOOK LIKE THEIR TACTICS, GORIN-SUNN.

LET'S REGROUP BACK AT H.Q. I WANT TO KNOW WHAT HAPPENED HERE.

"...THERE'S SOMEONE YOU'RE GOING TO WANT TO WELCOME BACK."

I'M NOT ONE TO QUESTION A 'RIXIAM, BUT THIS FEELS...RISKY.

EASY, JASKER. THEY'RE *THE LAW*. THEY WON'T ATTACK WITHOUT PROVOCATION.

SHUNK

PRIXIAM!

SHUNK

SHUNK

SHUNK

DOWN!

DRAGGING THE CORPS' NAME THROUGH THE MUD. *OPEN WAR.* ALL THE *DEATH.* JUST TO END UP *RIGHT BACK* WHERE YOU STARTED.

AFTER I ESCAPED YOUR PRISON, I SHOULD'VE KEPT RUNNING. AVOIDED THIS ENTIRE *CURSED* VENTURE.

WAS IT WORTH IT?

YOU'RE GOING ABOUT IT ALL WRONG. *CONTRITION.* THAT'S HOW YOU GET THE GUARDS ON YOUR SIDE.

I'M SEEKING *PAYBACK,* NOT PENANCE. THE OUTER CLANNS WERE PROMISED A NEW FOOTHOLD IN EXCHANGE FOR OUR EXPERTISE.

DEALS WERE STRUCK. *SERVICES* PERFORMED. BUT THE DURLANS NEVER PLANNED ON DELIVERING. THEY COULDN'T EVEN MANAGE TO KILL OFF YOU *DAMNABLE* SHERIFFS.

A UNIVERSE WITHOUT GREEN LANTERNS. IT'S A POPULAR IDEA THESE DAYS.

BUT AT LEAST THE CORPS *TRIES* TO DO RIGHT.

IT *FAILS.*

I FAILED!

BUT I'M *LEARNING*. *YOU* SHOULD'VE LEARNED THAT AN *ENTIRE GROUP* DOESN'T DESERVE TO BE PUNISHED FOR A *LEADER'S* MISTAKES.

I'VE LEARNED IT'S BETTER TO STAY UNDERGROUND. LEAVE THE *BRIGHT LIGHT* OF WAR TO THOSE THAT KNOW IT BEST.

WHICH BROUGHT ME BACK TO YOU. WE *BOTH* HAVE REPUTATIONS AT STAKE HERE IN THIS FIGHT. SO LET'S *BARTER.*

ALWAYS WORKING AN *ANGLE*, RIGHT? TOO BAD YOU'VE GOT NOTHING I WANT.

THE KHUND MILITARY IS *CRUSHED.* ALL YOUR FIGHTERS ARE EITHER *DEAD* OR IN OUR *JAIL.*

NEXT STOP: DURLA. THEN THIS MESS WILL BE *OVER.*

YOU WON'T FIND THE DURLANS ON THEIR HOMEWORLD. YOU WON'T FIND THEM AT ALL. NOT WITHOUT HELP.

THIS WAR WAS NEVER ABOUT JUST ELIMINATING THE CORPS. THAT WAS ONLY THE *SALES PITCH* THE DURLANS USED TO GET THE OUTER CLANNS AND THE KHUND TO TAKE THEIR SIDE.

IT WAS ALWAYS ABOUT *POWER.* POWER ENOUGH TO RULE *EVERYONE.* NOW, WITH THE WAR HAVING TAKEN ITS *TOLL* ON *ALL* SIDES, EVERYONE WILL BE THAT MUCH EASIER FOR THE DURLANS TO RULE.

UNLESS SOMEONE *STOPS* THEM.

SEE, DURLAN PHYSIOLOGY IS *UNSTABLE.* IT TAKES *ENERGY* FOR THEM TO CHANGE FORM. CONSUME ENOUGH, THEY CAN *LOCK* THEIR FORM.

THIS RACE OF BEINGS THEY FOUND-- THESE *DAXAMITES,* WHOEVER THEY ARE-- THE DURLANS WANT TO BECOME THEM. *PERMANENTLY.*

AFTER THE WAY THEY *DOUBLE-CROSSED* ME TODAY, I'M STARTING TO WONDER IF THAT MIGHT NOT BE A GOOD THING.

LUCKILY, THEY CAN'T DO IT WITHOUT *A LOT* OF ENERGY.

A *VAST* SUPPLY OF *CONSUMABLE* POWER. *POTENT,* TOO. NOT EASY TO COME BY.

YOU KNOW WHERE THE *ENERGY SOURCE* IS, DON'T YOU.

DO I DETECT A *CRACK* IN YOUR CONFIDENCE? A FEAR THAT MAYBE--JUST *MAYBE*--YOU HAVEN'T PLANNED FOR EVERY CONTINGENCY?

I TACKED ON A HEFTY *FINDER'S FEE* BEFORE GIVING THE DURLANS THAT INFORMATION.

NATURALLY YOU DIDN'T CONSIDER FINDING OUT *WHY* THEY WERE WILLING TO PAY SO MUCH.

LIKE, MAYBE BECAUSE IF THEY CAN BECOME DAXAMITES, THEY'LL BE DAMN NEAR *INVINCIBLE.*

AND NOW WE COME TO OUR BARGAIN. I'LL GIVE YOU THE LOCATION, BUT I GET TO HELP YOU FIGHT THE DURLANS.

WHEN THEIR GREAT GAMBIT GOES UP IN SMOKE, I WANT THEM KNOWING *I* PULLED THE TRIGGER. *NOT* FIGURATIVELY.

IF YOU'RE WASTING MY TIME, THE *DEEPEST, BLACKEST* HOLE IN THE UNIVERSE WILL BE COZIER THAN THE CELL I LEAVE YOU IN.

THE ANSWER'S BEEN IN FRONT OF YOU ALL ALONG.

HOW MANY OF MY CLANN HAS HE LOCKED UP? HOW MUCH *BUSINESS* HAS *HE* COST US?

A BEING OF LIVING ENERGY, FROM AN *OCEAN* OF THE SAME.

GORIN-SUNN...

THE DURLANS ARE HEADED FOR *ZEZZEN...*

"HIS PEOPLE DON'T STAND A CHANCE..."

I COULD WAIT NO LONGER... TO GAZE UPON IT.

EONS OF SEARCHING, BROTHERS AND SISTERS...NOW THE ERA OF OUR SUPREMACY IS ALMOST COME.

I KNOW NOT WHO YOU ARE, ODD BEING. BUT YOU'RE UNWELCOME ON THE SHORES OF MY KINGDOM.

DEPART.

THEN IT IS YOUR REIGN THAT WILL WITNESS THE SEA OF GENERATIONS CONSUMED TO ITS FINAL DROP.

TAKE HEART IN KNOWING THAT NONE OF YOUR SUBJECTS WILL BE LEFT TO SCORN YOU.

BLUB BUBBLL

UPRISING PART 4: INSIDIOUS

VAN JENSEN writer BERNARD CHANG & MORITAT artists MARCELO MAIOLO colorist
cover art by BERNARD CHANG & MARCELO MAIOLO BOMBSHELL variant cover by ANT LUCIA

PEOPLE OF DAXAM, YOU'RE IN *GRAVE* DANGER...

R'AMEY HOLL   ASH-PAK-GLIF   VOLK   REES-VAN   MUKMUK   MALET DASIM   CHERNISS   KWAAL   VON DAGGLE   SALAAK

STAND DOWN, JRUK.

YOU DAXAMITES ARE AMONG THE MOST POWERFUL BEINGS IN THE UNIVERSE WHEN EXPOSED TO A YELLOW SUN. BUT YOUR SUN IS RED. WE CAME TO PROTECT YOU.

TELL HIM, PROLLET. WE NEED NO HELP.

AS HE SAID, WE DAXAMITES HAVE LEARNED TO PROTECT *OURSELVES.* YOU LANTERNS HAVE CAUSED ENOUGH DAMAGE HERE.

HOW DARE YOU CHALLENGE OUR HONOR--

--IT WAS THE *SINESTRO CORPS* THAT ATTACKED DAXAM. YOU XENOPHOBIC FOOLS *KNOW* THE SACRIFICE I MADE TO LIBERATE YOU.

LANTERNS! IF YOU HAVE BUSINESS HERE...

...YOU WILL ADDRESS M--

SODAM... YOU ARE ALIVE?!

FATHER?

I...THOUGHT YOU WISHED ME DEAD. I SWEAR, I DON'T POSSESS THE *ION ENTITY...* I CANNOT MAKE OUR SUN YELLOW AGAIN.

THIS DOES NOT MATTER, SON. I AM SO *HAPPY* TO HAVE YOU BACK!

I'M SORRY TO INTERRUPT, BUT WE DON'T HAVE MUCH TIME. SHAPE-SHIFTERS CALLED *DURLANS* ARE COMING HERE TO *REPLICATE* YOU ALL.

THIS SUN MAY BE RED, BUT THE UNIVERSE HAS *MILLIONS* OF YELLOW ONES. THE DURLANS AIM TO USE DAXAMITE POWER FOR CONQUEST. *NO PLANET* WILL BE SAFE.

WE'VE LEARNED FROM THE PAST. DAXAM IS PREPARED TO DEFEND ITSELF.

THE SOLDIERS ARE BUT ONE LINE OF DEFENSE.

COME. I WILL SHOW YOU. LET THE OTHERS STAY HERE AND REST.

YOU SHOULD NOT BE HERE, DAGGLE.

I UNDERSTAND THAT LANTERN STEWART HAS VOUCHED FOR YOU, BUT WE ARE AT WAR WITH THE DURLANS--*YOUR* SPECIES. AND YOU YOURSELF HAVE SAID THAT WE SHOULD *NEVER* TRUST A DURLAN.

YOUR SENSES ARE AS *SHARP* AS I REMEMBERED, SALAAK.

I WANTED TO KNOW HOW THE WAR IS GOING.

WE'VE LEARNED THAT THE DURLANS PLAN TO EXTRACT ENERGY FROM THE PLANET ZEZZEN.*

I HAVE TRIED TO ALLOW THE RINGS TO HOME IN ON DURLAN DNA, BUT IT SEEMS IMPOSSIBLE.

GREEN LANTERN #32.--INFOMAT

MY PEOPLE *HAVE* NO TRUE DNA. IT SHIFTS EVERY TIME THEY CHANGE FORM. IT'S WHY THEY HATE THEMSELVES--THEY HAVE NO TRUE SELF. I FEAR THIS WAR WAS A FEINT, AND THE TRUE PRIZE IS THE DAXAMITE FORM.

ASK YOURSELF SOMETHING, WOULD THEY WAIT UNTIL THE *LAST MINUTE* TO SECURE THEIR PRIZE?

SLUROOK

BUT THAT WOULD MEAN--

I'M SORRY, SALAAK.

FFFFF

I DON'T HAVE TIME TO EXPLAIN, BUT I NEED TO ACCESS THE RING CHAMBER.

≥KAFF≤
≥KAFF≤

SSLURRRRK

SWORE I'D NEVER WEAR THIS AGAIN.

⟨GHKK⟩

GREEN LANTERN OF SECTOR 700 RECOGNIZED.

SYSTEM OVERRIDE CONFIRMED. RING PROGRAMMING INTERFACE ONLINE.

EXTRACTION SEQUENCE INITIATED. COMMAND EXECUTE IN 3... 2...

SORRY, SALAAK. I WISH IT DIDN'T HAVE TO BE THIS WAY.

EXTRACTION BEGUN.

SSRKKRRL

AAAAGGGHHHH--!

THIS IS **MADNESS**, FATHER. YOU'RE **WEAPONIZING** OUR PEOPLE.

IT WOULD BE MADNESS NOT TO **USE** THE POWER INTRINSIC TO OUR DNA, NOT TO UTILIZE OUR GREAT ABILITIES.

IT WAS **YOU** WHO SHOWED US THE WAY, SODAM. IF YOU HAD NEVER LEFT DAXAM AND BEEN **EXPOSED** TO YELLOW LIGHT, WE WOULDN'T HAVE LEARNED OF THE **STRENGTH** HIDDEN INSIDE US.

OUR ARMY HAS BEGUN BOARDING THE SHIPS. FATE HAS RETURNED YOU IN TIME TO JOIN THEM.

IF YOU DO THIS, YOU'LL BRING MORE ATTENTION. YOU'LL MAKE **MORE** ENEMIES.

HOW IRONIC OF A GREEN LANTERN TO ARGUE AGAINST **INTERVENTION.** SHOULD DAXAM **CEDE CONTROL** OF OUR PLANET, LET YOU **DICTATE** OUR FATE?

WE DON'T WANT TO **CONTROL** DAXAM. WE WANT TO **PROTECT** YOU, SO THAT YOU CAN BE **FREE** TO LIVE AS YOU CHOOSE.

SODAM... YOU CAN'T JOIN THEM.

NO, ARISIA. WHATEVER COURSE THEY PICK, MY PLACE ISN'T AT THEIR SIDE. I NEVER SHOULD HAVE COME BACK.

YOU'RE QUITE RIGHT ON THAT LAST COUNT, **SON.**

BUT AS TO YOUR PLACE, I'M AFRAID YOU HAVE NO CHOICE IN THE MATTER.

ENOUGH TALK. THESE SOLDIERS HAVEN'T BEEN **CHARGED UP.** LET THEM SEE HOW THEY FARE AGAINST A STAR SAPPHIRE.

HAPPY TO FIGHT AT YOUR SIDE, FATALITY.

NO. WE CAN'T FIGHT THEM.

FINALLY, YOU UNDERSTAND, LANTERN STEWART.

ZZZKKKASSSKK

"THERE WILL BE
NO VICTORY FOR
YOU HERE."

-:NNNNNGH:-

GGRAAAAHHHH--!

SSKKRRRAAKKLL

EXTRACTION
COMPLETE.

DAGGLE...

WHAT IS
THIS?

UUHHHHHNN--

RINGS
UPDATE
INITIATED.

THE
RINGS--

WHAT
HAVE YOU
DONE?!

EVERY DURLAN...
WAS INFECTED WITH
RADIATION. THROUGH
MY RING...THE SYSTEM
DUG INTO MY CELLS. IT
IDENTIFIED THE
ISOTOPE...

RING DATABASE UPDATED.

DURLAN DETECTION ENABLED.

DURLANS? BUT HOW--?

HOW COULD THEY--?

WELL, THEN, THE PRETENSE IS POINTLESS NOW. YOU DID NOT ARRIVE HERE *EARLY*, LANTERNS. YOU WERE *TOO LATE.* THE BATTLE FOR DAXAM WAS ALREADY FOUGHT--

--AND THE DURLANS WON.

SLURRRK

WHERE IS MY FATHER?!

WHEN WE *INFILTRATED* DAXAM, I ABSORBED YOUR FATHER'S DNA WITH A SINGLE *HANDSHAKE.* NO ONE NOTICED WHEN I TOOK HIS PLACE IN THE SENATE.

OUR MISSION WASN'T TO *IMPERSONATE* DAXAMITES. WE ARE *REPLACING* THEIR RACE.

WHEN OUR AGENTS STOLE YOU FROM ZARDOR, YOU GAVE US A VISION OF A GREAT NEW FUTURE. DURLAN AMBITION MARRIED TO DAXAMITE STRENGTH!

BEFORE I *GUTTED* YOUR FATHER, I TOLD HIM THAT ALL OF THIS-- THE *DOWNFALL* OF DAXAM--WAS *BECAUSE OF YOU.*

NO...HE WAS *RIGHT*...IF I'D NEVER LEFT HOME, MY PEOPLE WOULD NEVER HAVE BEEN DISCOVERED...

YOU SHOULD BE PROUD. AS DAXAMITES, WE WILL RULE *ENTIRE* GALAXIES. AND IT WILL BE LANTERN YAT THAT LEADS OUR *GREAT ARMY* INTO BATTLE.

WHAT--?

ENOUGH! WE WILL LIBERATE THE UNIVERSE FROM YOU!

FOR THE *ATROCITIES* YOU'VE COMMITTED HERE, YOU AND THE REST OF YOUR KIND ARE GOING TO SPEND THE REST OF YOUR *NASTY LIVES* LOCKED IN A CELL.

ATROCITIES?!

THOOOOOM

WHO ARE **YOU** TO DELIVER JUDGMENT, LANTERN STEWART? WHERE IS THE **VENGEANCE** FOR THE PEOPLE OF XANSHI?

NNNGH--

WHAT OF THE **SUFFERING** YOU LANTERNS INFLICTED UPON **MY** PEOPLE? I LIVED THROUGH IT. I SAW MY PLANET **BURN!**

THE DURLANS WHO DIDN'T ESCAPE ARE SECURED.

WE HAVE TO JOIN HAL AND THE REST OF THE CORPS AT ZEZZEN. THEY'RE SERIOUSLY OUTGUNNED.

I WON'T BE GOING.

WE NEED *EVERY* LANTERN TO FIGHT, SODAM--YOU MORE THAN ANYONE, WITH YOUR POWERS.

IF EVEN *ONE* DURLAN REACHES THE SEA AND ABSORBS THAT POWER...

NO.

THIS IS *MY* FAULT. BECAUSE OF ME, THE DURLANS LEARNED OF MY PEOPLE'S EXISTENCE. AND NOW...

WE DAXAMITES ARE TOO DANGEROUS. WE MUST STAY HIDDEN. WE MUST *ALL* REMAIN HERE.

YOU'VE GIVEN PLENTY TO THE CORPS. IF THERE'S ANYTHING WE CAN DO--

GO.

AND MAKE THEM *PAY*.

UPRISING PART 5: LAST STAND OF THE LANTERNS
ROBERT VENDITTI writer BILLY TAN penciller MATT BANNING, ROB HUNTER and JAIME MENDOZA inkers ALEX SINCLAIR colorist
cover art by BILLY TAN & ALEX SINCLAIR BATMAN 75TH ANNIVERSARY variant cover by ETHAN VAN SCIVER & ALEX SINCLAIR

THE COMMAND CENTER.

IT'S *GENOCIDE*, HAL. THE DURLANS SLAUGHTERED HALF THE DAMN *PLANET* AND COPIED THE DAXAMITES' DNA.

NO...

THEY'RE TRYING TO *SHAPE-SHIFT* THEIR WAY INTO BECOMING A *MASTER RACE*. IT'LL BE SUPERMAN TIMES A *THOUSAND.* EXCEPT, YOU KNOW, *EVIL.*

ALL THAT *SUPED-UP* STRENGTH WILL BE WAY TOO MUCH FOR THE DURLANS TO *MAINTAIN,* UNLESS THEY INGEST ENOUGH *ENERGY* TO HOLD THEIR FORMS.

IF THEY MANAGE TO DO THAT... WELL, THERE IS NO AFTER THAT.

I KNOW EXACTLY WHERE THEY'RE HEADED. OUR *ONLY CHANCE* IS TO BEAT THEM THERE.

BETTER THINK UP *ANOTHER* ONLY CHANCE, JORDAN.

SCANS SHOW A WHOLE *FLEET* JUST TOUCHED DOWN ON ZEZZEN.

MY GOD...

SOUND GENERAL ALARM, KILOWOG. EVERY LANTERN ON MOGO HAS TO GET TO ZEZZEN. *NOW.*

MEET UP WITH US AS FAST AS YOU CAN, JOHN...

"...WE'RE GOING TO NEED ALL HANDS."

SLUDRRRXXX

DO NOT TRY TO HOLD IT, ANCIENT.

UHNN...

BENEATH THE POWER OF THIS YELLOW SUN, THE STRAIN OF A **DAXAMITE** FORM IS TOO GREAT. YOU NEED--

DO NOT CODDLE **ME**. MY KIND ARE THE ANCESTORS FROM WHOM **EVERY DURLAN** IS SPAWNED.

I BROUGHT US TO THIS WORLD--

--TO THE SHORES OF THIS **ENERGY SEA** THAT WILL **WASH AWAY** GENERATIONS OF LIVING IN SHADOW.

ONCE WE DRINK DEEP, DURLANKIND WILL BE FOREVER IN THE SUNLIGHT. **RULERS** WITHOUT **EQUALS**.

ANCIENT!

THEY FOUND US!

"THE CORPS IS HERE!"

FORM THE **WALL!**

WE HOLD THIS GROUND! NO MATTER WHAT!

WHAT ARE YOU?

US? UM... WE'RE GREEN LANTERNS.

WE'RE GOING TO KEEP YOU SAFE.

WE KNOW WHAT A GREEN LANTERN IS.

GORIN-SUNN IS ONLY THE MOST FAMOUS ZEZZITE OF ALL TIME!

I'M SAYING WHAT ARE YOU? YOU'RE SO... DIM.

YOU'RE NOT THE FIRST GIRL TO TELL ME THAT.

I'M A HUMAN. FROM A FARAWAY PLACE CALLED "EARTH."

"ERF"?

SWIM NOW, DROPLINGS.

DIVE DEEP WITH THE OTHERS.

OKAY! BYE, GORIN-SUNN!

BYE, HUMAN FROM ERF!

TURN AROUND! TRAMPLE THE--

NNGH!

KRRGLLL

QUIT WHILE YOU STILL **CAN**, DURLAN.

YOUR **SIMPLE** STRATAGEMS CANNOT OUTWIT ME. MY MIND HAS SPANNED **MILLENNIA.**

MAYBE I HAVEN'T BEEN AROUND AS LONG AS YOU...

...BUT I DON'T HAVE TO BE A **GENIUS** TO SEE ONE PLUS ONE EQUALS--

ARRLLK!

HSSAKK!

LIKE SHOOTING FISH IN A *CREEL.*

ZZN

ZZN

ZZN

ZZN

ZZN

SPAKK

GAGGL

UPRISING PART 6: FATALE
VAN JENSEN writer BERNARD CHANG artist MARCELO MAIOLO colorist
cover art by FRANCIS PORTELA & TOMEU MOREY BATMAN 75TH ANNIVERSARY variant cover by SEAN CHEN & ALEX SINCLAIR

THEY CAME SO CLOSE...

BUT THEY DIDN'T WIN.

DON'T WORRY, YRRA--

--THE DURLANS WILL NEVER HURT ANYONE AGAIN.

I KNOW, JOHN. IT IS JUST... AS A *STAR SAPPHIRE*, THE SIGHT OF SO MUCH DEATH, SUCH HATRED, IT PAINS MY HEART.

THE WAR IS *OVER*. LET'S PUT IT OUT OF MIND. COME ON--I PROMISED YOU A BEACH VACATION...

...IT'S TIME I FINALLY DELIVERED.

EEEEEEEEEEEEEEE

WHAT THE HELL?

OH MY GOD!!

EEEEEEEEEE...

SLURRRRK!

THE LIMITLESS ENERGY THAT IS THE ZEZZITES...

WITH IT, A DURLAN CAN PERMANENTLY HOLD ANY FORM IT WISHES.

YOU... YOU WE NEVER

AND UNFORTUNATE FOR YOU--

...IT CAN'T BE. OU *LOVE* ME. THAT NG WOULDN'T BE ON YOUR HAND UNLESS--

UNLESS IT HAD BEEN *DECEIVED*... LIKE SO MANY OTHER RINGS.

TAKING ANOTHER'S SHAPE IS ONLY PART OF BEING A DURLAN. YOU MUST ALSO REPLICATE PERSONALITIES--AND *PASSIONS*.

WE--WE WERE... *TOGETHER*...

RING ERROR. UNAUTHORIZED WEARER DETECTED.

STAR SAPPHIRE YRRA CYNRIL LOCATED. REUNITING--

YRRA... SHE'S ALIVE.

CRUNCH!!

FATALITY IS *BURIED DEEP*, LANTERN STEWART--

--NOT THAT YOU'LL EVER FIND HER.

RING: TRANSMIT TO CORPS LEADER JORDAN.

HAL! WE WERE *WRONG!* IT'S *NOT* OVER--

THANK CUBALAYA THIS CONFLICT IS ENDED. I HAVEN'T HAD *LEAVE* IN MORE CYCLES THAN I CAN TALLY.

DO NOT VACATION-PLAN YET, PERDOO. THE DURLANS ARE DEFEATED, BUT THERE ARE *HUNDREDS* WE MUST GUARD, AND MOGO IS STILL IN PROXIMITY OF ZEZZEN.

IF *ONE* SLIPS LOOSE AND REACHES THE SEA OF GENERATIONS--

THE SENTIENT PLANET MOGO. MOBILE HEADQUARTERS OF THE INTERGALACTIC POLICE FORCE KNOWN AS THE GREEN LANTERN CORPS.

SKRRONK

STEL--!

0II0IIII0III0III

WHERE ARE MY PEOPLE?

:SQQAWWK:

FATALITY WHAT AR YOU--?

LET'S SEE IF I CAN'T *DIG* IT OUT OF YOU.

YIEEEE

HSSS

GHAA--!

NOW, THERE IS ONE *MORE* MISSION I HAVE BEEN TASKED WITH...

IS *THIS* THE CORPS' LAST LINE OF DEFENSE?

UNHH--!

PATHETIC.

FACE *ME*, DURLAN! I HAVE AN ESPECIALLY *NASTY* VARIETAL OF VENOM FOR YOU.

AH, OLIVERSITY. I KNOW *EXACTLY* HOW YOUR VENOM WORKS-- AND THAT YOU MUST LOWER YOUR PROTECTIVE AURA TO DELIVER IT.

DID YOU KNOW DAXAMITES CAN FREEZE ANYTHING WITH THEIR *BREATH?*

AND NOW TO FREE MY PEOPLE AND AT LAST CLAIM *VICTORY.*

RING STATUS REPORT. GREEN LANTERN 2111 DECEASED.

SECTOR 2111 SCAN FOR REPLACEMENT SENTIENT INITIATED.

IT'S OVER, *SISTER.* YOU WERE TOO LATE.

THE TRAITOR. *GOOD.* I WOULDN'T WANT TO LEAVE WITHOUT GIVING YOU THE DEATH YOU *DESERVE.*

WHAT--? WHAT HAVE YOU *DONE?!*

ONCE THE CENTRAL BATTERY'S COMPUTER IDENTIFIED THE RADIOACTIVE ISOTOPE THAT ALLOWS OUR KIND TO CHANGE FORM--

--MOGO SYNTHESIZED AN ELEMENT TO *COUNTERACT* IT.

NO... IT CAN'T BE. WE'RE... WE'RE SO *CLOSE--*

HOW COULD YOU DO THIS TO YOUR *OWN* KIND?!

EVERY DURLAN IS STUCK IN FLUX--*FOREVER.* THEY'LL NEVER TAKE ANOTHER FORM. YOU ARE ALONE.

I'LL KILL YOU FOR THIS!!

I'VE GOT HER.

COME ON... CLOSE THE GAP!

THAT SILLY CONSTRUCT ONLY SLOWS YOU DOWN, JORDAN.

TRUE--

"--BUT IT HAS MISSILES."

GRRRNNH!

JOHN, I CAN'T BEGIN TO IMAGINE...

I DON'T KNOW HOW I CAN SHOW MY FACE. I BROUGHT THE ENEMY RIGHT INTO OUR INNER CIRCLE. THEY KNEW *EVERY MOVE* BEFORE WE MADE IT...

HOW MANY *DIED* BECAUSE I SAW WHAT I *WANTED* TO?

SHE TRICKED *ALL OF US*, JOHN... AND SHE WASN'T THE *ONLY* ONE.

MAYBE, MAYBE NOT. BUT I CAN'T THINK ABOUT THAT NOW. THERE'S ONE LAST THING I HAVE TO DO...

THE *REAL* YRRA IS OUT THERE...

"...AND I'M NOT GOING TO REST UNTIL I *FIND* HER."

THE DURLANS *DAMAGED* THE CORPS...BUT THE LANTERNS DEFEATED THEM. *YOUR WAR* FAILED.

I...I AM SORRY NOT TO BRING BETTER NEWS.

DO YOU THINK THIS NEWS UNEXPECTED-- OR EVEN *PROBLEMATIC?*

AS THE LANTERNS FOUGHT BATTLE AFTER BATTLE, *OUR EMPIRE* HAS GROWN--*THE SHADOWS* NOW STRETCH ACROSS THE UNIVERSE.

WE *HARDLY* EXPECTED THE DURLANS TO DEFEAT THE LANTERNS, JUST WEAKEN AND DISTRACT THEM. WHAT THE CORPS HAS FACED SO FAR WAS BUT THE OPENING *SKIRMISH...*

OF COURSE, MY LADY. I APOLOGIZE--

THE FINAL *ECLIPSE* IS COMING...

...AND THE *SHADOW EMPI* SHALL BEAR WITNESS TO IT.

INCURSION

ROBERT VENDITTI writer **BILLY TAN & MARTIN COCCOLO** pencillers **MARTIN COCCOLO & ROB HUNTER** inkers **ALEX SINCLAIR** colorist
cover art by **BILLY TAN & ALEX SINCLAIR** SELFIE variant cover by **CRAIG ROUSSEAU & DAVE McCAIG**

"...IT'S GOING TO BE A SHORT TRIP."

SPACE SECTOR ZERO. THE SENTIENT PLANET MOGO

MOBILE HEADQUARTERS OF THE INTERGALACTIC POLICE FORCE KNOWN AS THE GREEN LANTERN CORPS.

AFTER THE UPRISING...

HOME SWEET HOME, AGARUSH-WHATEVER.

AGARUSHNAWOKLIAG.

THERE'S YOUR OLD WARDEN, VOZ. THOUGH I *SWEAR* I SENT HIM HOME ON *LEAVE* LIKE THE REST OF THE CORPS.

BESIDES, I'D RATHER WELCOME BACK CONVICTS LIKE *THIS ONE* PERSONALLY.

IF IT'S ALL THE SAME TO YOU, HAL, I WANT TO STAY AND BE SURE NOL-ANJ AND HER CLANN FIGHTERS ABIDE BY THE CONDITIONS OF THEIR PAROLE.

THEY HELPED US WIN THE WAR, BUT THAT DOESN'T MEAN THEY'RE *REFORMED.*

WHAT ABOUT YOU, SIMON? YOU'RE SUPPOSED TO STAY ON EARTH.

DOESN'T *ANYONE* FOLLOW ORDERS AROUND HERE?

I GOT CLEARANCE FROM GUY TO MAKE A RUN THROUGH *RED LANTERN* TERRITORY.

I LIKE THIS PLANET BETTER THAN YOUR OLD ONE, LANTERNS. IT'S MUCH MORE...

...EMOTIONAL.

KRAK

KR-KRK

MOGO! TURN DOWN THE WILLPOWER! HE'S *FEEDING* OFF IT!

I AM A PLANET, CORPS LEADER JORDAN. MY GEOLOGIC PROCESSES ARE A CONSTANT ACT OF WILL.

HE'S HERE! UNCLE HAL'S HERE!

JANE?! WHAT ARE YOU--?

STAY BACK ⸸URK⸸!

AAAAA!

OH MY GOD!

HOWARD! JANE! GET AWAY FROM THEM!

AAAAA!

NO! I DON'T WANT FEAR! AIGGH!

AAAAA!

AIGGH!

MOMMY! DADDY!

MAKE IT GO AWAY!

HAL! DO SOMETHING!

LOOKS LIKE IT'S ALREADY DONE.

AFRAID... SO AFRAID...

GET HIM TO THE POWER DAMPENERS INSIDE THE LOCKUP, VOZ. BEFORE HE HAS ANOTHER MOOD SWING.

MY PLEASURE.

KIDDOS?

...IS IT *GONE?*

JANE. HOWARD. IT'S SAFE NOW.

YOU GUYS PUT THE *FEAR* IN HIM. FOR REAL.

PROMISE? ⇒SNIFF⇐

PROMISE.

SEE? ALL CLEAR.

UNCLE *HAL!*

HAHA GOOD TO SEE YOU, TOO. YOU HAVE *NO IDEA.*

BUT A *HEADS-UP* WOULD'VE BEEN NICE.

CARE TO EXPLAIN THIS, SIMON? OR AM I SUPPOSED TO BELIEVE MY KID BROTHER AND HIS FAMILY TOOK A *GREYHOUND* TO THE MIDDLE OF *SPACE?*

ACTUALLY...

...THAT'S ON *ME,* PAL.

YOU SENT EVERYONE HOME ON LEAVE AFTER THE WAR, BUT...

...WELL, YOU *CAN'T* GO HOME NOW THAT GUY GARDNER'S *REDS* ARE IN CHARGE OF EARTH'S SECTOR.

SO I HAD LANTERN BAZ BRING A CHUNK OF HOME TO YOU.

YOU SHOULD'VE ASKED ME, KILOWOG. YOU KNOW THE REGULATIONS--NO FAMILIES ON MOGO. *SUPPORT STAFF* ONLY.

MR. KILLYWOG WANTED IT TO BE A SURPRISE!

SURPRISE!

I'M PROTOCOL OFFICER. IT AIN'T LIKE I'M GONNA WRITE MYSELF UP FOR *VIOLATING REGS.*

BESIDES, GUY CAN BE TRUSTED TO LOOK AFTER EARTH FOR A BIT. NO NEED TO HAVE A GREEN THERE *ALL* THE TIME.

I DON'T MIND MAKING THE TRIP, HAL. IT'S NICE TO SEE THE STARS A LITTLE.

I OWE YOU GUYS ONE. *TRULY.*

JUST TRY NOT TO FREAK OUT THE KIDS WITH THAT *MUG* OF YOURS, KILOWOG. THEY'VE BEEN STARTLED ENOUGH FOR ONE DAY.

NO WAY! HE'S LIKE A *GIANT BULLDOG,* BUT CAN GIVE *PIGGYBACK RIDES!*

SNORT
SNORT

MAYBE WE SHOULD HAVE SOME LUNCH. *INDOORS...*

AW, MOM! CAN'T WE KEEP *EXPLORING?* THERE'S SO MUCH *COOL STUFF!*

YEAH! COOL STUFF!

I'D APPRECIATE IT, MA'AM. WE DON'T GET LITTLE ONES 'ROUND HERE MUCH.

...

OKAY, A LITTLE WHILE LONGER...

BUT I'LL FEEL BETTER WHEN WE'RE BACK *HOME.*

ALL RIGHT!

LET'S GO SEE WHAT *SAINT WALKER* IS UP TO. I KNOW HE WOULDN'T WANT TO MISS MEETING *YOU* TWO.

KEEP *MOGO* IN THE CONVERSATION, SO HE DOESN'T *LOSE TRACK* OF YOU!

DID YOU SAY SOMETHING, CORPS LEADER JORDAN?

GAH! WHAT THE *HELL* WAS *THAT?!*

THAT'S THE PLANET. MOGO IS, YOU KNOW, *LIVING.*

LOOK AFTER MY FAMILY, MOGO.

I WILL GIVE THEM MY MOST FOCUSED ATTENTION.

THE PLANET *TALKS?!*

THE PLANET TALKS...

COME ON, LITTLE BROTHER. I THINK YOU NEED TO SIT DOWN.

A *DRINK* IS WHAT I NEED.

THAT, TOO.

KHUNDISH ALE. I GRABBED SOME AT A SPACEPORT. THEY COME IN *FIVE-PACKS*.

TRY AND WRAP YOUR HEAD AROUND *THAT*.

NO KIDDING?

KIND OF FIZZY, LIKE THOSE *POP ROCKS* JACK USED TO EAT BY THE HANDFUL WHEN WE WERE KIDS.

A LOT CHEERIER THAN THE RACE WHO BREWS IT, BELIEVE ME.

HAHAHA!

WHAT?

JACK AND I ALWAYS SAID YOU THOUGHT YOU WERE THE *CENTER* OF THE *UNIVERSE*. NOW--

--HERE YOU ARE.

IT ISN'T ALL IT'S CRACKED UP TO BE. BELIEVE ME.

NO? YOU LIVE ON A *TALKING PLANET*. YOU HAVE A *MAGIC RING* THAT LETS YOU DO PRETTY MUCH ANYTHING. YOU BUY YOUR *BEER* AT A *SPACEPORT*.

I DRIVE A *TAURUS* AND SHOP AT *7-ELEVEN*. TRUST ME, YOU'RE DOING ALL RIGHT FOR YOURSELF.

SEE, WHY CAN'T I HAVE *THAT* LIFE?

FOR A MINUTE, I THOUGHT YOU MIGHT. YOU AND *CAROL.*

WHAT HAPPENED THERE?

IT WASN'T WORKING OUT. OTHER FISH IN THE SEA, RIGHT?

THAT'S *ALL* YOU HAVE TO SAY ABOUT IT? EITHER YOU REALLY ARE AS TOUGH AS YOU LET ON...

...OR SETTLING DOWN--A FAMILY, A *NORMAL* CAREER-- ISN'T FOR YOU.

ONLY *YOU* KNOW THE ANSWER TO THAT.

HIGHER! HIGHER!

YOU MAKE A DARN GOOD SWINGSET, MOGO.

THANK YOU FOR THE COMPLIMENT, PROTOCOL OFFICER KILOWOG.

ISN'T HE *CUTE*, MOMMY?

THIS ONE IS A *SHE*, YOUNGLING.

SHE.

AA!

SHE *LIKES* YOU, MOMMY! DON'T WORRY. MR. WALKER SAYS THEY DON'T *BITE.*

TREEMUNKS ARE QUITE HARMONIOUS CREATURES.

HEY! CAN YOU PICK STUFF UP WITH THAT *HEAD* THING?

NO. VERY IMAGINATIVE OF YOU TO ASK, THOUGH.

OH, ALL RIGHT...

OKAY. I CAN TELL SOMETHING ELSE IS ON YOUR MIND. SPILL IT.

WHAT YOU SAID ABOUT THE RINGS...THEY AREN'T MAGIC. THERE'S SEVEN DIFFERENT LIGHTS THAT RUN ON SEVEN DIFFERENT EMOTIONS. GREEN FOR *WILLPOWER*, YELLOW FOR *FEAR*, VIOLET FOR *LOVE*...

THE ENERGY THE RINGS USE, IT COMES FROM A RESERVOIR. THE SAME SOURCE THAT SUPPLIES EMOTION TO *EVERY LIVING THING* IN THE UNIVERSE.

WHEN THE RESERVOIR RUNS DRY--WHICH *DAMN NEAR* HAPPENED A FEW MONTHS BACK--THE UNIVERSE *ENDS.*

WITH THAT KIND OF *COST*...HOW DO I KNOW? HOW DO I KNOW IT'S RIGHT TO USE A RING AT *ALL?*

YOU'RE SAYING MY CONSTANT WORRY THAT SOMETHING WILL HAPPEN TO SUE AND THE KIDS COMES FROM A *LIGHT POOL* SOMEWHERE?

I THOUGHT I GOT THAT FROM MOM.

I'M *SERIOUS*, JIM. I JUST GOT DONE FIGHTING A WAR AGAINST *WHO KNOWS* HOW MANY WORLDS THAT THINK THE GREEN LANTERNS ARE *PARASITES.*

AND HERE'S THE THING: *THEY MIGHT NOT BE WRONG.*

THAT'S YOUR BIG DILEMMA? I HATE TO BREAK IT TO YOU, BUT *LIFE* IS CONSUMPTION.

WE *BREATHE.* WE *EAT.* WE *BUILD HOUSES* FROM TREES, ON LAND THAT USED TO BELONG TO LITTLE FURRY CRITTERS.

THE QUESTION ISN'T *WHETHER* YOU CONSUME. THE QUESTION IS WHAT YOU *DO* WITH WHAT YOU USE.

WHAT *YOU* DO IS BE A *HERO.*

ASK ME, THAT'S WORTH THE TRADE-OFF.

SO WHAT HAPPENS WHEN THERE'S ONLY ONE BEER LEFT, AND WE'RE BOTH STILL THIRSTY?

KNOWING THE KHUND, WE'RE SUPPOSED TO FIGHT TO THE *DEATH* FOR IT.

GRANT ME ONE REQUEST?

SHOOT.

NEXT TIME YOU FIND YOURSELF IN A WAR, DON'T THINK ABOUT IF IT'S RIGHT FOR YOU TO FIGHT.

THINK ABOUT ME AND SUE AND THE KIDS.

THINK ABOUT ALL THE PEOPLE ON ALL THE WORLDS EVERYWHERE-- I CAN'T BELIEVE I JUST SAID *THAT* WHO DON'T HAVE WHAT IT TAKES TO DO WHAT YOU DO.

BECAUSE I MAY BE JUST A GUY FROM COAST CITY, BUT I KNOW THIS: BIG AS THE UNIVERSE IS--

START AT THE BEGINNING!

GREEN LANTERN
VOLUME 1: SINESTRO

GREEN LANTERN CORPS VOLUME 1: FEARSOME

PETER TOMASI FERNANDO PASARIN SCOTT HANNA

RED LANTERNS VOLUME 1: BLOOD AND RAGE

PETER MILLIGAN ED BENES ROB HUNTER

GREEN LANTERN: NEW GUARDIANS VOLUME 1: THE RING BEARER

"GEOFF JOHNS HAS TURNED SINESTRO, GREEN LANTERN'S FORMER ENEMY, INTO A THREE-DIMENSIONAL CHARACTER... FASCINATING."
— THE NEW YORK TIMES

GEOFF JOHNS DOUG MAHNKE

START AT THE BEGINNING!

GREEN LANTERN CORPS
VOLUME 1: FEARSOME